The Planets

Your Mission to Uranus

by Christine Zuchora-Walske
illustrated by Scott Burroughs

Content Consultant
Diane M. Bollen, Research Scientist,
Cornell University

magic Wagon

visit us at www.abdopublishing.com

Published by Magic Wagon, a division of the ABDO Group, 8000 West 78th Street, Edina, Minnesota, 55439. Copyright © 2012 by Abdo Consulting Group, Inc. International copyrights reserved in all countries. All rights reserved. No part of this book may be reproduced in any form without written permission from the publisher.

Looking Glass Library™ is a trademark and logo of Magic Wagon.

Printed in the United States of America, North Mankato, Minnesota.
052011
092011

 THIS BOOK CONTAINS AT LEAST 10% RECYCLED MATERIALS.

Text by Christine Zuchora-Walske
Illustrations by Scott Burroughs
Edited by Holly Saari
Series design and cover production by Becky Daum
Interior Production by Christa Schneider

Library of Congress Cataloging-in-Publication Data
Zuchora-Walske, Christine.
  Your mission to Uranus / by Christine Zuchora-Walske ; illustrated by Scott Burroughs.
      p. cm. — (The planets)
  Includes index.
  ISBN 978-1-61641-683-6
  1. Uranus (Planet)—Juvenile literature. I. Burroughs, Scott, ill. II. Title.
  QB681.Z83 2012
  523.47—dc22
                                2011010661

Table of Contents

Imagine You Could Go

Nobody has ever traveled to Uranus. It doesn't have enough oxygen for you to breathe. Its bitter cold would freeze you solid.

Imagine if you could be the first to travel to Uranus.

Uranus is the farthest planet from Earth you can see without binoculars or a telescope. Uranus is very dim in the night sky, though. It is a blue-green dot about as big as a period on this page.

Solar System

As you travel, you take out your map of the solar system to find your way. The map shows eight planets orbiting the sun. Uranus is the seventh planet from the sun.

Distance from Earth

Uranus is about 1.7 billion miles (2.7 billion km) away from Earth. You are traveling that distance on a super speedy rocket. Still, it will take you about nine years to get to Uranus! Good thing you packed enough books and games to keep you busy.

CHESS

CHECKERS

BEDTIME STORIES

SPACE SPACE

WATER

BONE

URANUS

EARTH

BONES

WATER

Size

You read about Uranus during the long trip. It is much bigger than Earth. About 63 Earths would fit inside it. It is as heavy as 14 Earths.

Uranus is less dense than Earth. The particles that make up Uranus are less tightly packed together than the particles that make up Earth. Earth is mostly rock. Uranus is mostly gas and liquid.

Years and Days

One year is the time a planet takes to orbit the sun once. One Earth year is 365 days. One Uranus year is 84 Earth years. Thank goodness you weren't born on Uranus. You would have to wait 84 years for your first birthday party!

All planets spin like tops. Most are tilted as they spin. Uranus is tilted a lot. It looks like it is on its side as it spins.

As each planet spins, it turns toward the sun and then away from the sun. One full spin equals one full day, from sunrise to sunrise. A day on Earth is 24 hours.

On Uranus, the time between sunrises depends on where you're standing. This is because of how much the planet tilts. On the equator, each new sunrise comes every 17 hours. At the poles, a sunrise comes every 42 Earth years.

Appearance

Finally, your spacecraft gets close to Uranus. You look out the window. Clouds surround the planet. Methane, a type of gas, makes them look blue-green. You remember reading that methane is a common fuel on Earth.

Atmosphere

You travel through the atmosphere. It is denser than Earth's. Your instruments tell you the atmosphere is mostly hydrogen and some helium. These are the same gases that make up the sun.

Hold on! Your rocket is coming into some strong winds. Wind speeds on Uranus can reach 360 miles per hour (580 km/h). That's much stronger than Earth's strongest hurricanes.

Uranus's atmosphere has water vapor and ammonia. Ammonia is a compound used in fertilizers on Earth.

Temperature

Uranus is one of the coldest places in the solar system. Temperatures can drop to –364 degrees Fahrenheit (–220°C).

The pressure increases as you fly closer to the planet. This feels like you're diving deeper and deeper into a lake on Earth.

Uranus's gravity is just a little weaker than Earth's. So, your body feels just a little lighter on Uranus than it does on Earth.

Liquid Layer and Core

As you keep flying closer, you press the button that turns your craft into a submarine. You've come to an ocean of liquid water, methane, and ammonia. You dive deep into the ocean. Thousands of miles down, you reach the planet's core.

No one knows exactly what the core is made of. Scientists think it's rock. Is that true? You'll report your findings back on Earth.

Rings

You turn your craft around and head upward. You leave the ocean and clouds behind. It's time to explore Uranus's rings.

Thirteen rings circle Uranus. The rings are mostly made of dust. But there are chunks of rock and ice in the rings, too. You steer carefully around the rubble so you don't crash.

Moons

You still have time to explore Uranus's moons. The planet has 27 of them! The moons are made of ice and rock.

You land on the biggest moon, Titania. It is 981 miles (1,579 km) wide. This is less than half as big as Earth's moon. Good thing you brought your sunglasses. Frosty patches reflect sunlight and make Titania very bright.

Heading Home

You've made important discoveries on Uranus. And, you've seen amazing sights. But you traveled for years to get there. You still need to make a long trip home.

You turn your spacecraft toward the sun. You can't wait to return to Earth.

How Do Scientists Know about Uranus?

Uranus is dim, and it moves very slowly through Earth's sky. It's hard to see, and its orbit is hard to notice. So for centuries, people thought Uranus was just another star in the sky.

In 1781, William Herschel discovered Uranus with a telescope. He named the planet Georgium Sidus (George's Star) after England's King George III. But other scientists did not like the name. They agreed to name the planet Uranus, after the ancient Greek god of the sky. Herschel discovered two of Uranus's moons, Titania and Oberon, in 1787. For the next two centuries, scientists continued to study Uranus through telescopes.

In 1977, scientists accidentally discovered nine of Uranus's rings while watching a star pass behind Uranus. In August of that year, scientists launched *Voyager 2*, the only spacecraft to study Uranus at close range. *Voyager 2* flew by Uranus in January 1986. The spacecraft discovered ten small new moons, two new rings, and a strange magnetic field. Over the next 20 years, scientists found more small moons and two more rings using the Hubble Space Telescope.

Uranus Facts

Position: Seventh planet from sun

Distance from sun: 1.8 billion miles (2.9 billion km)

Diameter (distance through the planet's middle): 31,763 miles (51,118 km)

Length of orbit (year): 84 Earth years

Length of day (from sunrise to sunrise): 17 hours at the equator, 42 Earth years at the poles

Gravity: About one-tenth weaker than Earth's gravity

Number of moons: 27

Words to Know

atmosphere—the layer of gases surrounding a planet.

core—the center of a planet.

dense—made of material that is tightly packed together.

gas—a substance that spreads out to fit what it is in, like air in a tire.

gravity—the force that pulls a smaller object toward a larger object.

methane—odorless, colorless, flammable gas that reflects blue light.

orbit—to travel around something, usually in an oval path.

solar system—a star and the objects, such as planets, that travel around it.

water vapor—water in gas form, or steam.

Learn More

Books

Landau, Elaine. *Uranus.* New York: Children's Press, 2007.

Whiting, Sue. *Ancient Orbiters: A Guide to the Planets.* Washington DC: National Geographic, 2006.

Yasuda, Anita. *Explore the Solar System!* White River Junction, VT: Nomad Press, 2009.

Web Sites

To learn more about Uranus, visit ABDO Group online at **www.abdopublishing.com**. Web sites about Uranus are featured on our Book Links page. These links are routinely monitored and updated to provide the most current information available.

Index